D1461902

EARLY DAYS ON THE ROAD
A Photographic Record
of Hull and the East Riding

compiled by

Ted Dodsworth

HUTTON PRESS
1987

Published by the Hutton Press Ltd.
130 Canada Drive, Cherry Burton, Beverley
East Yorkshire HU17 7SB

Copyright © 1987

No part of this book may be reproduced, stored in a
retrieval system or transmitted in any form, or by any
means electronic, mechanical, photocopying, recording
or otherwise without the prior permission of the
Publisher and the Copyright holders.

Printed by Clifford Ward & Co. (Bridlington) Ltd.
55 West Street, Bridlington, East Yorkshire
YO15 3DZ

ISBN 0 907033 52 0

Easington Wes. S.S. Trip, July, 1906.
Lister's Series 021

Upwards of 80 members of the Easington Wesleyan Methodist Sunday School attended the chapel's outing to Withernsea in July, 1906, with the local farming community providing the transport for the day. In this view of the excursion can be seen a Foden traction engine towing in tandem a pair of Wolds farm waggons accompanied by a horse and rulley supplied by William Tennison, farmer and carrier of Kilnsea.

ACKNOWLEDGEMENTS

The Author wishes to thank the following for their invaluable assistance in the preparation of this book: the staff of the Kingston upon Hull Record Office and of the Local Studies Library, the Central Library, Hull; John Bradshaw, the Curator, and staff of the Hull Museums and Art Galleries, particularly for the photograph on the back cover; and the research staff of the National Motor Museum at Beaulieu.

INTRODUCTION

The camera, in popular use from the 1880s, flourished at the turn of the century with the introduction of the Post Office approved picture postcard. Local studios thrived as the popularity of photographic postcards increased. A collecting fervour for cards depicting every conceivable subject grew throughout the country, a demand that was to last until well after the First World War. It is due to this collecting phenomenon that much local history material has survived for the present-day collector. In compiling this first volume of pictures from his personal collection, the author has tried to present a representative selection of early road users from Hull and the East Riding. The photographs show the vehicles and people in their contemporary settings, providing an incidental commentary on changing fashions in clothes, architecture and roads during the period 1895 to 1925.

Ferry crossing point (East Bank), Ferry Lane, Stoneferry, Hull. Dating back to the middle-ages, a crossing or 'Stone Ford' was recorded on or near to this site.

FERRY-BOATS . . .

Final ferry crossing from West Bank.

Industrial expansion in the Stoneferry district at the turn of the century necessitated a more direct link between the two banks at this point on the River Hull. Striving to contend with increased traffic, the ferry was finally withdrawn c.1904, the present road bridge connecting Ferry Lane with Clough Road opening in October 1905.

Today with the ever-increasing volume of traffic now crossing Stoneferry bridge, it is soon to be replaced by a larger span within the very near future.

1909. Police Constable Herbert Hobson of the East Riding Constabulary, on bicycle patrol accompanied by a lady cyclist, approaches the Wawne landing after crossing the River Hull in the smaller of the two ferry-boats. P.C. Hobson was resident in Wawne for a number of years.

On the bank side stands the Windham Arms public house; the landlord and ferryman at this time and for several years later was Mr. Donald Brewer.

... AND WATERMEN

About six miles north from Hull, the Wawne ferry plied the River Hull serving the villages of Thearne on the west bank and Wawne to the south. The ferry had over a long period of time been operated by successive tenants of the public house known as the Windham Arms, which was situated adjacent to the Wawne landing stage on the south bank, as may be seen in the accompanying photograph. The ferry service ceased to operate in 1947. Local opposition to the closure resulted in a request to the borough council that the service be reinstated. It appears that due to legal difficulties the appeal came to nothing, for as far as is known the ferry has not worked since.

c.1912. Navigating the River Hull in full flood, members of the Holderness Hunt and ladies out cycling cross from the direction of Thearne by pontoon ferry toward the Wawne landing at the Windham Arms.

Penny Farthing racing machine, *c.*1895. Location believed to be the Athletic Ground, Boulevard, Hull. The cyclist is thought to be J. W. Stocks, a Hull postal clerk and local sporting personality. In 1893 he claimed the credit of being the first cyclist to cover twenty-five miles within the hour on a safety cycle.

The penny farthing was more commonly known as the Ordinary, first appearing in 1870 with an estimated 50,000 machines on the English roads by 1880.

Hull Cycle Parade, *c.*1920. Decorated penny farthing road machine and junior cycle. The popular nickname Penny Farthing originated in the mid-1880s, about the time the design was being superseded by the modern Safety cycle. The junior model depicted carries the slogan 'Follow Me And Ride A Bicycle.' Newbridge Road cycle dealer Matthew Robson and son Frank pose for the camera before the start of the parade.

East Hull rag and bone merchant Walter Gillot with decorated handcart, *c.*1914.

FOOTWORK

Walter Gillot, trade card.

'Marine Store Dealer. Best prices given for Rags, Bones, Old Iron, &c, :: Best prices for Hare and Rabbit Skins. Postcards receive prompt attention. Distance no object.'

Delivery tricycle, *c.*1903. Scales and Sons Ltd., boot and shoe makers, Carr Lane, Hull, 1903 to 1933.

MILKO!

Above: Newland dairyman and float, *c.*1906. Location the Hull Bank district between Newland and Dunswell. This area consisted mostly of dairy farms supplying a large proportion of Hull's milk. The milk float depicted illustrates a further example of E. S. Annison coachwork.

Top, left: Milk roundsmen handcarts, Riley's Dairies of Hull, Bridlington railway arches depot, *c.*1913. 'Pure ice cold milk delivered any area Bridlington twice daily,' so ran Riley's slogan.

Bottom, far left: Dairy float 1909, John Dixon, dairyman, and Mrs. Dixon outside their Temple Street address, Hull. Coachwork by E. S. Annison, Witham, Hull.

Left: Milkman and handcart, *c.*1898, location Great Thornton Street, Wesleyan Chapel, Hull. Milk was usually ladled into each customer's own container by measuring can straight from the churn in the days before the introduction of the modern glass bottle delivery system.

Village pump, Sancton, near Market
Weighton. Horse-drawn water
carriers, c.1905. It is likely that fresh
water was delivered in this manner
in the days before mains water
supply.

W. Slater, general carrier, Warter,
Pocklington and Driffield. *c*.1900,
Driffield.

HORSE POWER

Market gardener or small-holder's
light cart, Endike Lane, Cottingham
district, *c*.1906.

Timber waggon, Horsley Smith & Co., Hedon Road, Hull. Show horse and exhibition log load, *c.*1909.

Decorated parade float 'Jacobs Cream Crackers,' 1909. Horse and rulley provided by William H. Prince, carters agent and carrier, Prince Street, Hull.

Pony and light rulley ready for deliveries in the service of Joseph Stephenson, beer retailer and general grocer. Premises on the corner of Short Street and Spencer Street, central Hull (1919 to 1930). Demolished in the 1930s to make way for the building of the Ferensway Coach Station and Hull City Transport Central Garage, Lombard Street, the entrance to which is now situated on the site of Stephenson's former shop.

Kilnsea school children arriving for classes at the Elementary School, Dimlington Road, Easington, 1908. Conveyance by private omnibus provided by William Tennison, local farmer and carrier. A horse bus service was operated by Mr. Tennison up until 1945 serving Easington, Kilnsea and Spurn. Easington and District School opened in 1876 for 120 children and is today functioning as a Primary School under the direction of the Church of England, older children attending at Patrington.

RURAL RIDES

A mixture of bedecked transport, comprising horse-drawn wagonette, motor char-a-banc and horse and trap, parade through the streets of Hornsea during the Coronation festivities of George V, 1911.

Blue Bell Inn, Sproatley, on the Hull to Aldbrough road. For the thirsty traveller the inn offered its services as a free house and as headquarters for Hull cycling clubs. Pony and trap driven by James Crawforth, proprietor of the Blue Bell, 1911.

Sporting a straw boater and button-hole, Yeast Merchant Arthur Pullan and young companion pose with the firm's horse and delivery van, Somerset Street, Hull, *c.*1908.

Park Street, Hull, *c.*1910. The Davidson family pony and trap, young Maurice Davidson taking the reins. In later years Maurice became a fancy goods wholesaler trading as Moisha's, Waverley Street, Hull.

Hull Brewery draymen, *c*.1910, Silvester Street, Hull.

Butter and provision importer Stanley Cartwright, Grafton Street, Beverley Road, Hull, 1908. Of special note is the splendidly groomed grey mare and well turned out grocer's van.
In 1919 Mr. Cartwright turned his attention to hotel keeping, becoming proprietor of the Manchester Hotel, George Street, Hull.

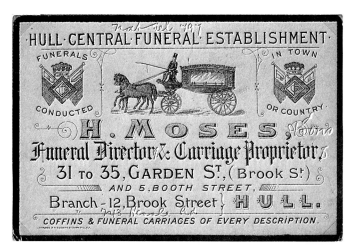

A LOCAL UNDERTAKING

Left: Calling card, Henry Moses & Son, funeral directors and carriage proprietors (1882 to 1972).

Below: H. Moses, bow-ended hearse, *c*.1906. The magnificent black stallions specially imported from Belgium were generally known to undertakers as the 'black brigade.'

H. Moses, closed funeral carriage drawn by black Belgians was advertised by the proprietors as Silent-Tyred Washington Cars, *c.*1906.

H. Moses, Clarence wedding carriage pulled by a fine pair of white Dutch or Belgian horses and driven by liveried coachmen, *c.*1906.

A WINTER'S TALE

Left: Three in hand wagonette-brake on hire from Robert Winter, carriage proprietor, Charles Street, Hull, 1911. Members of the Sportsman hotel fishing club, Hedon Road, Hull, assemble for a day's outing.

Below: Crowded with happy trippers eagerly anticipating the day ahead, Robert Winter wagonettes about to depart from Reform Street, Hull, *c.*1920.

The wagonette made an ideal vehicle for a large party to take a trip to the country or seaside as it had the advantage of ample storage space under the seats or down the middle of the floor for picnic baskets or hampers.

A surviving example of the wagonette-brake can be seen at the Museum of Transport, High Street, Hull.

DAY TRIPPERS

Sunday School outing, *c.*1905. A Yorkshire Waggon is the day's transport provided by farmer Ryby Wright, the Manor House, Humbleton near Hedon. Location believed to be Hedon. The Yorkshire Waggon illustrated is of the Wolds model, a type popular in the Holderness region. A similar example is to be seen at the Museum of Rural Life, Beck Isle Museum, Pickering, North Yorkshire.

A cool and breezy Withernsea greets the arrival of a Sunday school trip, *c.*1910. Conveyance for the day has been supplied by an unidentified carrier from Roos.

FARES PLEASE!

Hull Street Tramways car No.17 trundles along Beverley Road, passing May Street as it journeys towards its Newland destination, c.1895. By 1899 the privately owned Hull Street Tramways system had been taken over by the Hull Corporation and operated as a municipal undertaking.

Horse-drawn omnibus Victoria, Sutton to Hull service, 1905. The route was operated by Mr. Brian Lazenby, omnibus proprietor and resident of Sutton, with buses departing daily from the Duke of York public house, Sutton, running via Stoneferry and terminating at the White Horse Hotel, Carr Lane, Hull. The horse bus Victoria is pictured standing in Leads Road adjacent to Stoneferry Green en-route for Hull. An omnibus of this type was able to seat up to twenty-eight passengers and average a speed of seven to eight m.p.h. Of special interest is the advertisement 'Murleys for Purifying Feather Beds,' Charlotte Street, Hull.

Dairycoates tram terminus, Hessle Road, Hull, 1907. A Hull Tramways electric car stands ready to start its return journey to Hull's city centre. Going in the opposite direction a horse-drawn omnibus heads towards Hessle village. Two separate operators provided a horse bus service between Hessle and Hull, Frederick Owbridge and George Henry Mann, both residents of Hessle. Horses for the service were stabled at the Granby Inn, Southgate, Hessle.

The North Eastern Railway had originally intended to take over the proposed route of the North Holderness Light Railway; however, in 1903 the N.E.R. opted instead for a bus service, starting at Beverley and calling at Leven, Brandesburton, North Frodingham and Beeford. Three Stirling 14-seat motor buses were purchased by the N.E.R. for the service at a cost of £898 each.

The arrival of two of the buses, seen here near the Black Swan in Brandesburton, appears to have aroused the curiosity of the local villagers.

OFF THE RAILS

North Eastern Railways Durkopp bus, *c.*1905.

Railways on the Road

Rain-soaked but not downhearted, a summer shower does nothing to dampen the spirits of passengers aboard a North Eastern Railways summer tour excursion from Scarborough, seen here arriving at Pickering, c.1910.

The vehicle illustrated is one of a pair of Hallford 34-seat char-a-bancs operated by the N.E.R. as part of their extensive touring fleet.

North Eastern Railway's Riverside Quay, Hull, *c.*1913. A N.E. railway policeman checks his watch as rulleys of the Lancashire and Yorkshire Railway Company wait in line to complete the loading of recently landed cargo. The local depot of the L. & Y. was at the Goods Station, Railway Street, Hull, where stabling was provided for the Percheron dray horses preferred by the L. & Y. as they were better suited to local stone sett roads.

Operating in less than ideal conditions a heavily laden Londonderry steam wagon of the North Eastern Railway Company is seen here working on the N.E.R. docks, Hull, 1913. The steam wagon illustrated is the second of seven purchased by the N.E.R. from the Londonderry Steam Wagon Company of County Durham in the years 1905-1906.

Station yard, Driffield, 1914. A North Eastern Railway Durkopp bus and horse-drawn conveyances await the arrival of the next train. The bus standing in the yard is one of five of German manufacture purchased by the N.E.R. for use on their Beverley-Brandesburton-Driffield service. A closer view of an N.E.R. Durkopp from the original batch of five can be seen on page 24.

Workmen put the finishing touches to the recently opened New Monument Bridge, Whitefriargate, Hull, 1906. A mixture of traffic crossing the bridge includes a horse-drawn van belonging to the Great Central Railway Co.; a close-up of the same vehicle can be seen on the opposite page.

Great Central Railway Company parcels delivery van, fleet no.38, seen standing outside the company's depot at the Railway Dock goods station, Kingston Street, Hull, c.1908. To be noted is the van's poster informing the public that the G.C.R. was able to offer 'Improved Service of Trains from and to Hull, Paragon Station,' for Liverpool, Manchester, Sheffield and Barnsley. Also to be observed is a young lady peeping out of the window seemingly intrigued by the cameraman photographing the railway staff.

The Yorkshire Agricultural Show of 1922 was held on the recreation fields, Anlaby Road, Hull. The Hull Daily Mail newspaper's representation at the show included this mobile advertisement in the guise of a colourful white and blue painted Ford van, a new addition to the paper's delivery fleet.

A more recent event was the celebration in 1985 of the 100th anniversary of the publication of the Hull Daily Mail.

'The Press Gang,' Bridlington, c.1914. Believed to be local press photographer H. D. Bolsover and friends enjoy a joke while straddling an overloaded Hull Daily Mail Triumph motor-cycle and side-car.

CROSSROADS

Anglo Villa, *c.*1908, former turnpike toll bar house Wyton Holmes at the junction of the Bilton, Sproatley and Preston roads. With the abolition of turnpike roads in the 1870s the Wyton Bar toll keeper's house was sold in 1879 to Hull builder William Brumby, and subsequently used as a private residence, the building realising £100. In later years the substantially built dwelling was used as the headquarters of the Wyton Bar Cycling Tourist Club, the building eventually being demolished in the 1930s/1940s.

The Park Street Barracks, Hull, was the headquarters of the 2nd East Riding of Yorkshire Royal Garrison Artillery (Volunteers). A gun detachment of the R.G.A. is seen here on parade at the garrison's Park Street drill ground, commonly known as Corporation Field, c.1900.

HORSE SOLDIERS

A column of Hull Royal Garrison Artillery (Volunteers) Heavy Battery horse artillery headed by a field workshop wagon proceeds towards summer camp held in July 1906 at Paull Point Battery on the River Humber.

'Breaking step' at the White Horse Inn, Ottringham, July 1905. Gunners of the 2nd East Riding of Yorkshire Royal Garrison Artillery (Volunteers) halt their journey at Ottringham to rest and water the horses, and, after taking liquid refreshment themselves, prepare to couple the teams up to the guns of the Heavy Battery in readiness to resume the garrison's march from Hull to summer camp at Kilnsea on the East Coast. The horses used by the R.G.A. were customarily loaned by local Hull businesses.
Anyone interested in historical army conveyance can view an impressive display of original military vehicles at the Museum of Army Transport, Flemingate, Beverley.

O.H.M.S.

'On His Majesty's Service' sign hung on the radiator of a 15 h.p. Star open tourer staff car indicates that the vehicle was probably involved in a military exercise of the period, *c.*1911. The driver and officer occupants of the motor car are members of the East Riding Royal Garrison Artillery, Territorial Force, Hull.

The serpent's head motor horn seen here on the Star was a novel car accessory, popular with early motorists.

Patrington 1913, 'On Manoeuvres.' An officer and men of the 4th Battalion East Yorkshire Regiment (Cyclists) Territorials carry out a training exercise taking them through the village of Patrington. Transportation of the Terriers is by cycle and a Bradbury motor-cycle combination with trailer. Headquarters of the regiment was at the Londesborough Street Barracks, Hull.

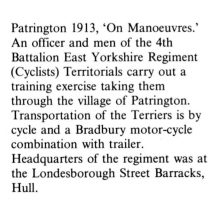

Members of the Hull Royal Garrison Artillery (Volunteers) Heavy Battery and Rifle companies arrive at camp accompanied by cyclists of the 2nd Battalion East Yorkshire Regiment (Rifle Volunteers), *c.*1903.

Staff Sergeant E. L. Miskin and men of the 5th Battalion East Yorkshire Regiment (Cyclists) H Company Territorials pictured at their Drill Hall H.Q., Hornsea, *c.*1908.

Mr. Charles Riley, proprietor of Riley's Dairies, Campbell Street, Hull, pictured with recruits, N.C.O.s and transport officer of the Royal Army Medical Corps on the occasion of the handing over of a Field Ambulance converted from a former dairy lorry owned by Riley's Dairies. Evidence would suggest that Mr. Riley presented the ambulance to the R.A.M.C. as a patriotic gesture in 1914. The Medical Corps was represented in Hull by the 3rd Northumbrian Field Ambulance with headquarters at the Wenlock Barracks, Walton Street.

Horses of Section 1 'A' Squadron East Riding Yeomanry (Wenlock's Horse) entrained at Hull ready for transportation by N.E.R. livestock wagons to the Yeomanry's summer camp, *c*.1913. Section horses receive last minute feeding and watering before departure.
Headquarters of the Hull and Holderness Squadrons, East Riding of Yorkshire Yeomanry, was situated at Railway Street, Beverley, with a riding school provided at Walton Street, Hull.
A permanent exhibition of items connected with the East Riding Yeomanry can be seen at the Sewerby Hall collection, Bridlington.

Orderly room staff of the East Riding Yeomanry at summer camp, Scarborough (Stepney Road), June 1913. A young trooper strikes an appropriate pose leaning against his Triumph motorcycle. In the background can be seen a large horse-drawn pantechnicon used to transport tents and other equipment to the camp site.

TAXI!!

Sitting in a gleaming East Riding registered Sunbeam, driver Charles Wilson waits patiently to collect his passengers from the next train to arrive at a local railway station, *c.*1912.

City and County of Kingston upon Hull.

REGULATIONS

FOR

Motor Hackney Carriages.

1908.

Reproduction from the cover of a copy of Hull motor-cab regulations, 1908.

High summer, 1910. Noon on a hot cloudless summer day on the forecourt of the N.E.R. railway station, Beverley. Crowding the area is a variety of public and private transport waiting to pick up passengers; identified amongst the assembled vehicles are hansom cabs, wagonettes, a landau and a solitary Darracq motor-cab registered to the Provincial Motor Hiring Co., Anlaby Road, Hull.

Left, top: A Belsize motor-cab and driver belonging to George Richardson, cab proprietor, Paragon Station, Hull, photographed near to the main entrance of the North Eastern Railway's Royal Station Hotel, Hull, 1910.
Established in the 1880s, Richardson's are today still in the taxi business with an office and cab rank only a few yards away from the scene of this picture.

Left, bottom: The Land of Green Ginger, in Hull's old town, is the setting for this view of Robert Vokes' Belsize taxi-cab, the first motor-cab operated by the Vokes in 1913.

Printed stationery of Robert and Clara Vokes, cab proprietors, Hull, 1880 to 1939.

Left, bottom: Madge, driver for Robert and Clara Vokes, pictured at their Beaumont Street stables, Hull, 1913.

Right, top: A splendidly turned out Clarence bridal coach pulled by a handsome pair of horses, 'Colonel' and 'May,' photographed at the Vokes office and residence, Beaumont Street, Hull, June 1912.

Right, bottom: Paragon Station cab rank, Hull, *c.*1908. Cab hire proprietor G. Richardson was the owner of this light type Growler able to seat upwards of four persons.

WEDDING
BELLES

Blundell's Yard, Beverley Road, Hull, c.1922. Decorated with traditional wedding day ribbons, a Renault bridal cab on hire from Charles Sellar, Hall Street, Hull, poses for the camera at Blundell and Spence's yard prior to escorting the waiting bride to church.

'Society Wedding' at the Church of St. Helen, Ladywell Gate entrance, Welton, c.1915. Adding the finishing touch to a special occasion, a spotless Daimler limousine waits as the happy bride is helped into church.

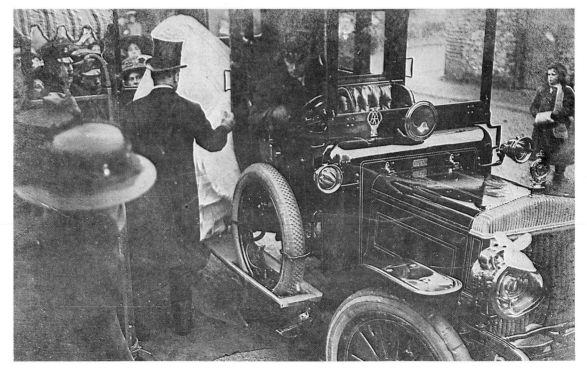

Holding open the door of an immaculate Unic motor-cab, an officer of the East Riding Constabulary waits for the bride and groom to have their photograph taken before ushering the newlywed couple to their seats. Location of picture believed to be the Kirkella area, *c*.1911.

*c.*1895, Mallison's Smithy. Muddy and unsurfaced, Cottingham Road viewed towards the Beverley Road and Clough Road junction. The open door to the left of the picture was the entrance to J. Mallison, blacksmiths, with the Haworth Arms public house to the right of the row of cottages.

A CHANGE
OF SCENE . . .

*c.*1905, a rural-looking Cottingham Road, Newland. Within a few short years the greatly improved road surface was to see the appearance of modern tramlines. In keeping with the times, Mallison's blacksmith premises was able to offer the new motorists, repairs, accessories and 'Pratts Motor Spirit.'

c.1910. Five years separate this view of Cottingham Road from the previous scene. Among the many changes already visible are Mallison's workshop demolished and the appearance of tramlines and cables radiating from the recently opened Cottingham Road tram depot, necessitating the cutting back of the tree line. The tempo of increasing road activity is highlighted by the presence of a motor-car, cyclists and delivery van.

COTTINGHAM ROAD

c.1925, modern Cottingham Road is now a broad suburban thoroughfare bounded by a thriving shopping and residential area, little changed up to the present day. Gone are the cottages and original Haworth public house, cleared to make way for an enlarged Haworth Arms, built in an imitation Tudor style much in vogue in the 1920s. Save for the policeman on point duty and an orderly boy road sweeper 'following the horses' it appears to be a quiet day on the road.

Hull City Corporation Tramways offices, Queens Dock Chambers, Alfred Gelder Street, Hull, decorated for the Coronation of George V, 1911. The site of the former tramways offices is presently occupied by the Burtons building, a prominent landmark situated at the corner of Whitefriargate and Princes Dock Street.

CITY OF HULL
TRAMWAYS

c.1925, a Hull Tramways open balcony car on service 'P' (Pier via Alfred Gelder Street), stationary in front of the L.N.E.R. ferry booking office, Nelson Street, Hull. Operating from 1903, the pier tram service continued over the years until 1931 when the route was taken over by motorbus; the service finally ceased after the withdrawal of the Humber ferry service following the opening of the Humber Bridge in 1981.

1905, St. John's Street, Victoria Square, terminus for services 'D' (Dairycoates), Hessle Road and 'A' (Anlaby Road) trams. The Dairycoates route proved to be the last operated in Hull by tramcar, the final car running in June 1945; all other tramway services had by this time been turned over to trolleybus and motorbus operation.

A group of curious children gaze with interest at the patriotically decorated trams, dressed overall in celebration of the Coronation of George V, 1911. Pictured at the Wheeler Street stage, Anlaby Road service car No.127 was one of a batch of tramcars built at the Hull City Tramways Liverpool Street works, Hessle Road, 1909/10.

Above: Aberdeen Street tramways depot, Holderness Road, Hull, *c.*1910. Motorman, tram guard and inspector pictured with tramcar No.112, built in 1903 by G. F. Milnes of Wellington, Shropshire. The Holderness Road service was inaugurated in 1900, extending to Aberdeen Street in 1903.

Top left: Cottingham Road, Hull, Saturday August 18th, 1906. 250 children and adults of the Olive Branch Lodge of Juvenile Free Gardeners travelled by tramcar to Newland for the lodge's annual day's outing. Amongst the aims of the Free Gardeners society was the provision of sick pay and medical attendance for children and adult lodge members.

Left: Spring Bank service tramcars arriving and departing at the Newland Avenue, Cottingham Road terminus, Hull, *c.*1905.

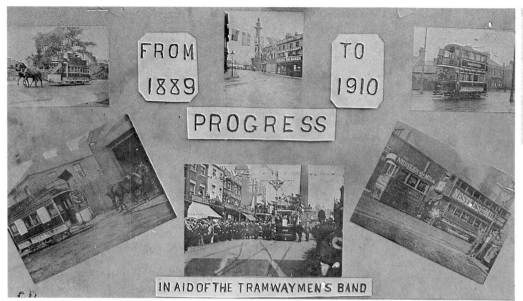

FROM 1889 TO 1910

PROGRESS

IN AID OF THE TRAMWAYMEN'S BAND

HULL TRAMWAYMEN'S BAND.

Third Annual Concert

At QUEEN'S HALL

Thursday, 9th Oct. 1919, at 7-30· p.m.

Above: Invitation to attend the Hull tramwaymen's third annual concert at the Queen's Hall, Alfred Gelder Street, Hull, 1919.

Left: Postcard souvenir produced by Charles Dyson, former tram guard and motorman, in aid of the Hull Tramways Bandsmen sick fund, 1910.

Below: Bandmaster and bandsmen of the Hull tramwaymen's band, 1919.

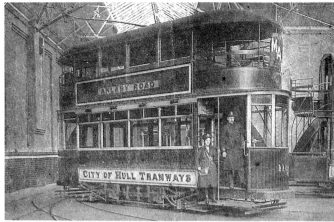

*Above: c.*1920 view of Hull Tramways inspector, motormen and conductors from the Marfleet depot, Hedon Road.

*Top: c.*1918, displaying a mixture of destination boards, tramcar No.118 is seen here with the motorman and conductress standing on the car's platform in one of the tramway's depots. Recruitment of women was encouraged in order to take up the duties of tramwaymen away on war service.

*Left: c.*1920, Marfleet Avenue (Service 'MA'), Hedon Road tram terminus, Hull. Car No.96 manufactured in 1901 by Hurst Nelson was rebuilt as fully enclosed between 1920 and 1931 with a final rebuild *c.*1933 as a single-deck works car and snow-plough.

Left: December 1904, in a Christmas card setting, snow-covered open-top tramcars are seen arriving at the Inglemire Lane request stop on the Hull Tramways Beverley Road service.

*Far left, bottom: c.*1903, Hull tramcar No.100 pictured at the Endike Lane terminus on the Beverley Road route, Newland. Car No.100 was built in 1901 by Hurst Nelson with further rebuilds in the 1920s and 1930s.

Below: Newland, open and closed-top tramcars on the Beverley Road service approaching the junction of Cottingham Road and Clough Road, *c.*1904.

Hull tramcar No.84 standing with its crew at the Endike Lane terminus on the Beverley Road route, *c.*1905. Car No.84 was unusual in that it was one of several open-topped cars originally purchased by Hull Tramways for operation as unpowered trailer cars in 1899. The lack of success with trail-cars quickly resulted in their withdrawal and they were subsequently rebuilt as standard power-cars. An early modification to car '84' was the fitting of Kennington roll-top roof covers in the period 1903/05, as seen in the above illustration. The moveable top covers were soon discarded in favour of permanent roof coverings as it was evident that conductors were taking more time in adjusting roofs and windows than they were in collecting fares.

Stoneferry Green, *c.*1910. Hull City Tramways Saurer omnibus, one of six purchased unused from the Mersey Railway Co., Birkenhead. Following many requests from Wilmington and Stoneferry residents, a bus service was introduced in 1909 operating from New Cleveland Street, Witham, via Wilmington, terminating at Stoneferry Green. The service although popular proved to be short lived, being withdrawn in 1912 due to high vehicle maintenance costs. Omnibus photographed near to the Premier Oil extraction mill works entrance, Ann Watson Street, Stoneferry Road.

LINE BUSES

Market Green, Cottingham, *c.*1924. On a tranquil sunny day in the neighbourhood of King Street, a Fussey's motor bus is seen waiting to depart to Hull from outside the Duke of Cumberland public house, Market Green. Up until the late 1920s Cottingham resident Tom Fussey operated a half hourly bus service daily from Cottingham to Hull.

'VICTORY' AND 'SPRINGVILLE'

A brace of Daimlers provide the day's transport for passengers travelling on a day trip into the country with Hessle tour operator J. B. McMaster, c.1923. McMaster's Daimler vehicles depicted include a torpedo-bodied char-a-banc and a landaulette taxi-cab.

Charles Street, Hull, c.1924. Preparing to leave with a party of club members from the County Hotel, Francis Street, is an Atlas bus supplied by Springville Passenger Services, Hessle.

Victory was the trade name originally adopted by Hessle bus operator Joseph McMaster for his fleet of passenger vehicles, two of which are seen on a family outing to Welton village in 1922. Pausing near to the Green Dragon public house, a Commer bus is pictured in the company of a char-a-banc manufactured by Daimler, a marque favoured by McMaster's. Both vehicles were new additions to the company's fleet in 1921/22.

Photographed within the Beverley area, a lady motor-cyclist riding an East Riding registered machine poses with a class of Sunday School children on an outing in 1909.

LADIES AND GENTLEMEN

Above: Pictured with members of the Kemp family is their recently acquired motor-cycle fitted with a wicker-chaired sidecar. East Riding, *c.*1919.

Oval, right: Reversed cap, goggles and weatherproof clothing suggest that this Hull motor-cyclist is ready for a fast day's touring on his 3 h.p. Triumph, *c.*1911.

Pearson Park, Hull, is the location for cycle dealer George H. Parker of Pryme Street, Hull, pictured with his wife about to move off to a local Autocycle Club rally riding a Rover Imperial 3¾ h.p. tri-car. Rover was one of a number of manufacturers to build forecar or tricar vehicles. The advent of the motor-cycle sidecar, first patented in 1903, hastened the demise of the tri-car as a form of transport by about 1910.

Brantingham Dale was the venue for Hull Autocycle Club's hill climb event, c.1906.

'Ready for the Road' is this proud owner of an East Riding registered Triumph motor-cycle, *c*.1905.

Shell-Mex motor spirit advertisement heading from invoice stationery used by George Ashton, cycle and motor dealer, King Street and South Street, Cottingham, 1925.

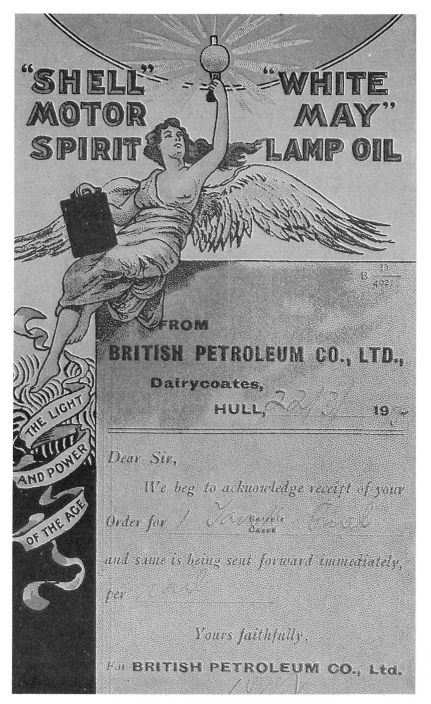

BEHIND THE WHEEL

'Good Companions,' Hull dye and chemical merchant, George H. Best with friends, seated on his 1911 12 h.p. Darracq. The unusual item fitted under the Darracq's running board appears to be a stone slab, the weight of which presumably was an effort in assisting the car's smooth-treaded tyres to obtain extra grip.

Illuminated postcard acknowledging an order for a tank of fuel to be forwarded to a Leeds customer by the British Petroleum Co., Dairycoates, Hull, 1915.

Light traffic crossing Monument Bridge includes a solitary motor-car making its way towards Queen Victoria Square, Hull, 1907.

1910, a pastoral Elloughton Dale disturbed only by a visiting motor-car, observed by a couple sitting by the roadside, their young child seated in a fashionable baby carriage.

*c.*1909, a stop-watch start for speed trials competitor No.14, Herbert Field of Hull, as he makes a dash for his Scottish manufactured Argyll touring car. Photograph location thought to be Brantingham Dale, a popular venue for local motoring clubs' road events. Speed trials on public roads were legal prior to 1925.

FUN . . .

AND GAMES

Hull publican John Walton driving an Argyll attempts to negotiate a village fête obstacle course, *c.*1909.

Westella, 1906. Hull fish merchant John McCann and daughter pictured in a two-seater Humberette enjoying a run into the country.

Out on his rounds, Hedon doctor James Soutter is pictured behind the wheel of his two-cylinder Humberette, c.1905. Accompanying Dr. Soutter is believed to be Mr. Walter Mendham. A resident of Souttergate, James Soutter was mayor of Hedon between the years 1896 to 1903, serving a total of five terms of office.

Members of the Snowden family relaxing at Withernsea in their new Vulcan open tourer. This handsome vehicle with its grey paintwork and red leather upholstery was first registered in 1911 to Hull boiler makers, Edwin Snowden Ltd.

A gentleman's carriage pictured on a crisp winter's day in Beverley, c.1909. Muffled up against the cold, chauffeur Charles E. Wilson looks out from his open driving position of a Daimler limousine, registered to Alexander Smith of Swanland Hall. In later years the Daimler was to be converted into a lorry and used by Smith & Nephew, surgical dressing manufacturers, from their Neptune Street premises, Hull, c.1914.

Riders of the Holderness Hunt assemble at Sproatley for a meeting in March 1910. A variety of pony and traps are in attendance as well as a large chauffeur-driven Edwardian style limousine.

"UPSTAIRS, DOWNSTAIRS"

Motored down from Tranby Croft, Anlaby, a 1904 registered Wolseley touring car is pictured in the grounds of Riston Grange, Long Riston, having recently arrived with week-end guests of landowner Thomas Boyes Jackson J.P., occupant of Riston Grange. From an upper window the Boyes' family pet watches inquisitively as house party members dressed for the hunt prepare to move off. One of the riders in the hunting party is believed to be Mrs. Mary Wilson, wife of Hull shipping magnate Arthur Wilson. Mrs. Wilson was the owner of the cream and black painted Wolseley.

Affectionately nicknamed 'Topsey' by his owner, this East Riding registered Argyll motor-car is seen in the vicinity of the East Yorkshire Regiment depot, Victoria Barracks, Beverley, 1913.

A smartly turned out Singer roadster pictured with hood raised against possible bad weather. Displaying a 1912 Hull registration number, this attractive two-seater, resplendent in its red enamelled coachwork, was latterly used by Thomas Nelson Driffield J.P., of Brafferton Manor, Helperby, Yorkshire.

'The dreaded sideslip' was a driving hazard not uncommon to the early motorist. Such a predicament has befallen a sporty two-seat Briton open tourer which has skidded off the road while out motoring in the North Cave area, c.1919. The driver, thought to be Mr. G. Laverack, a farmer of Drewton, near South Cave, looks pensively at the damage as he waits for help to arrive.

Superior workmanship and spaciousness are evident in this snapshot view of a five-seat 15.9 Vulcan, registered in 1920 to Harvey Ruddock of Hull. The lady in charge of this large vehicle is believed to be a member of the Ruddock family, well-known local wine and spirit merchants.

Pictured in Prestongate, Hessle, John W. Langley, a Hull fish merchant and Hessle resident, is seen with travelling companions riding in a 14/16 h.p. Argyll specially decorated to celebrate the 1911 Coronation of George V. Built in Glasgow, the Argyll motor-car was a make popular with many Hull and East Riding motorists.

Bleak House, Patrington, was the home of William Henry Coates, Medical Officer of Health to the Patrington Rural District Council. Dressed in the military uniform of an East Riding Volunteer, Mr. Coates is seen in the grounds to the rear of Bleak House about to climb into his 10 h.p. Humber runabout, *c.*1907.

With a driving position reminiscent of the days of horse-drawn travel, a chauffeur-driven electric landaulette town-car is seen gliding silently at speed along Bond Street, Hull, c.1908. Landaulette and Brougham electric-powered carriages enjoyed a brief spell of popularity in the Hull area. During the years 1905/1908 a total of eleven of these vehicles were registered, the majority for use as company cars to firms such as Reckitt and Son, Blundell and Spence, etc.

'Accommodation for Motors' was offered to the motor-car owner staying at Mr. Alfred Percy's York Commercial and Temperance Hotel, Anlaby Road, Hull. Seen standing in the roadway outside the hotel entrance is a Humberette two-seat roadster, fitted with wire-spoked wheels, c.1908. In later years the hotel was demolished to make way for the building of the present New York Hotel.

COMMERCIAL
BREAK

Manufactured in the U.S.A. by the Traffic Motortruck Corporation, St. Louis, Missouri, this imported example, with a van body fitted by a Hull coachbuilder, was added in 1923 to the delivery fleet of William Clayton, manufacturing confectioners, Walker Street, Hull.

William Clayton Ltd., Steam Toffee Works, Walker Street, Hull, works outing 1922. Employees of William Clayton pose for the camera before setting out on a day's outing, travelling by Grey Cars char-a-bancs. Grey Cars was a subsidiary of Riley's Dairies of Hull.

After travelling up from Hull, a Thornycroft van belonging to Needler's, the Hull chocolate manufacturer, makes a delivery to an account in Castle Street, Hinckley.

Motor Agent Gordon Armstrong publicity photograph taken in Pearson Park, Hull, of a 20 h.p. Ford Model T van before delivery to toffee and sweet manufacturer William Clayton of Walker Street, Hull, *c.*1922. The art of the coachbuilder is evident from the excellence of workmanship in the construction, paintwork and signwriting, testimony to the days of Hull's master craftsmen.

'Stop Me and Buy One' of our 'High Class Ices' would seem appropriate to this view of a Ford Model T ice-cream sales van, seen stopping off at a village within the Withernsea area, *c*.1925. The salesmen smiling for the camera may have stopped to change a flat rear-tyre, not an easy task to judge from the design of the ornate bodywork.

The pride of William Cussons Ltd., grocers and provision merchants, motor-van fleet on display in Blundell Street, Beverley Road, Hull, 1921. With the elementary school for a background, this specially posed line-up of Cussons' delivery vans includes makes by Ford, International, etc. Garaging for the vehicles was provided at Norfolk Street, to the rear of the company's main branch on Beverley Road, Hull. By the mid-1920s, William Cussons had a total of 30 shops and factories established throughout Hull and the East Riding.

Jameson Street, Hull.

The halcyon days that preceded the outbreak of the Great War in 1914 seem to be captured in this unhurried scene in Jameson Street, Hull, *c.*1913. Evocative of the period are the ladies dressed in fashionable clothes, possibly purchased at Costello's, the high-class ladies' outfitters situated on the corner of Jameson Street and Savile Street. Approaching from the direction of the outfitter's store, Costello's delivery van is seen making its way through the city centre.

Drypool, *c.*1908. Edward E. Chestney's horse and baker's van pictured near to the 'public baking' entrance of the Chestney bake-house in Church Street, Hedon Road, Hull. Established in 1903, Chestney's bakery continued to trade until the early 1940s.

New to William Jackson and Son confectionery department in 1908 was this 19cwt. Humber delivery van, decorated with signwriting which announced they were 'Tea & Coffee Specialists,' 'Bakers & Confectioners' and 'Bridecakes our Speciality.' The Humber van seen here outside the Jackson's Clarendon Street Works, Hull, was later to be 'called up' in 1914 by the War Office and saw service during the First World War.

'Cleanliness next to godliness' would seem to be an apt description as far as Allison's Steam Laundry was concerned, located as it was next door to a branch of the Salvation Army in Hawthorn Avenue, West Hull. A pair of Allison's horse-drawn vans, normally piled with wicker linen baskets, are specially posed to promote the laundry, *c.*1912.

Wearing freshly cut button-holes to complement their smart appearance, a driver and his assistant, laundrymen employed by Taylor's Laundry of Southcoates Lane, Hull, are observed in a relaxed pose with the laundry's recently acquired Commer delivery van. Finished in bright red and brown paintwork, the Commer was registered to Taylor's laundry in 1913.

Having completed the collection of a consignment of grain, a heavily laden Foden steam wagon prepares to return to the flour mills of Joseph and Benjamin Thompson, Dansom Lane, Hull, *c*.1916. Driver's labourer and driver pause for the camera before a final check and 'oil round.'

A frontal view of the Foden steam wagon illustrated on the previous page. With a wisp of steam drifting from the Foden's boiler safety valve, indicating a full head of steam, the grain wagon is seen ready to proceed on its return journey.

STEAM TRACTION

Prior to the opening in 1906 of the new Monument Bridge, Whitefriargate, Hull, an exercise to test the load-bearing potential of the recently completed bridge was carried out by the driving of a steam traction engine and trailer, hauling a heavy industrial type boiler repeatedly across the bridge.

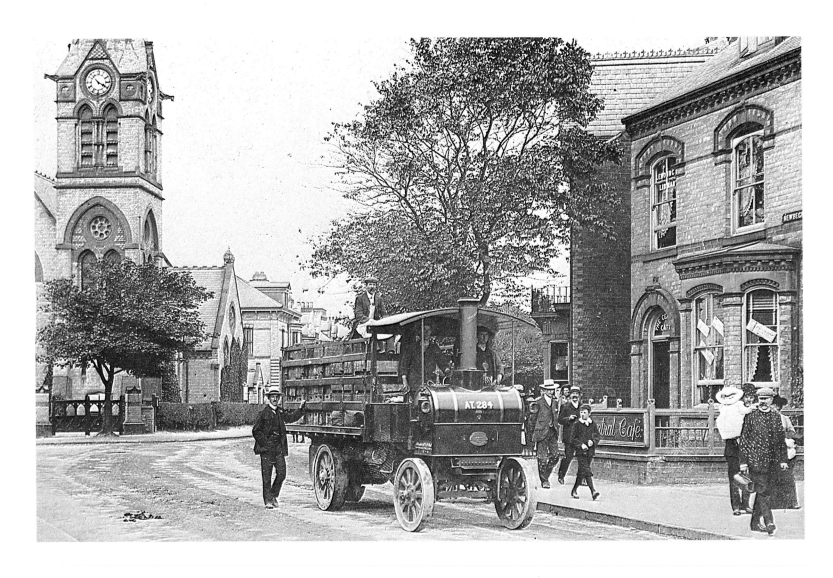

A Yorkshire Patent steam motor wagon owned by Hull mineral water manufacturer, James Hindle, is seen about to make a delivery to the Central Café, Newbegin, Hornsea, *c.*1905. Momentarily caught by the camera, men and machine are pictured at one of their many calls in this genteel seaside resort.

Alexandra Dock warehouses, Hull, *c.*1908, form the background to this view of a Foden steam lorry, contracted to Hull ship owners and underwriters Thomas Wilson and Sons.

c.1923, metal fatigue is thought to be the cause of a fractured steering fork on a Beverley Rural District Council's Aveling & Porter steam-roller, resulting in the machine's boiler coming to rest on the remains of its front roller. The apparatus fixed to the rear wheels appears to be a scarifier, a toothed attachment which could be lowered to break up the road surface before a new top dressing was laid down.

Traction Engine accident at Hessle. No 3.

ACCIDENTS
AND
REPAIRS

The owners, seen discussing the plight of their damaged traction engine, could well be asking themselves, "How do we get this lot back on to the road?" Pictured in the Hessle area, *c*.1905, the accident appears to be the result of heavy rain causing a slight road subsidence to tip the passing traction engine, coupled to a pair of gravel trailers, off the highway and down an embankment.

T. DRABBLE – ENGINEER,
RTH STREET. BRIDLINGTON WORKS.

A note on the reverse side of this postcard photograph of W. T. Drabble's engineering works, Bridlington, refers to 'A Traction Engine Hospital,' an apt description in view of the damage sustained in the two previous pictures. Members of Drabble's workforce pose with machines in for repair; a Fowler steamroller and an Aveling & Porter traction engine are seen 'receiving treatment.'

'With a little help from my friends.' Hammonds of Hull, furniture removals department, requires a helping hand to clear a path for their Sentinel steam wagon and pantechnicon trailer whilst attempting to climb a snow-covered hill on the western approaches to Hull, c.1914.

... ON DUTY

Loaded with bales of wool, a Sentinel steam wagon, No. 10 in Leopold Walford's Hull-based transport fleet, is seen in the proximity of a ship's bow, indicating the location as Hull docks, *c.*1921.

FIRE FIGHTERS

Meriting inclusion is this view of a Merryweather fire engine, recently delivered to the Scarborough Fire Brigade's central fire station, North Marine Road, North Riding, c.1914.

Striking a suitable pose for the camera at R. Spurr's Regent Terrace studios, Hull, c.1895, a mustachioed officer of the Hull Police Fire Brigade is photographed dressed in the uniform of captain. The highly polished helmet worn by the officer is a fine example of the many accessories supplied to Fire Brigades by the Merryweather Company, better known perhaps as fire engine manufacturers.

Captain, officers and firemen, volunteer members of the Hessle U.D.C. Fire Brigade are seen parading with their motor-pump fire appliance outside the brigade's fire station premises located in The Square, Hessle, c.1920s.

Worship Street Fire Station, Hull, *c.*1916. Casually standing, dressed in dungaree fatigues, a fireman of the Hull Police Fire Brigade appears with a fellow officer driving a cleaned and polished Dennis fire engine fitted with a wheeled escape ladder. Hand operated, the ladder was capable of reaching up to five storeys high. Able to reach a speed of 40 m.p.h., the Dennis was the second of this type of machine purchased for the Police Fire Brigade by the Hull Watch Committee in 1916.

Practice fire drill, Quay Road, Bridlington, *c.*1905. Volunteer firemen of the Bridlington Fire Brigade enjoy the fun as they carry out a practice fire alert in the Quay Road area, Bridlington. Set against the background of the North Eastern Railway's passenger station, the volunteers' horse-drawn fire appliance, a Merryweather steam-powered pumper, is seen taking water from a portable static-tank.

Pictured near the Northgate Station-House headquarters of the Cottingham Volunteer Fire Brigade, Captain Naylor and his men proudly pose with the brigade's Merryweather manual pump fire engine, *c.*1890s. Purchased in 1887 by the 'Local Board,' the Merryweather was housed 'at the ready' in a converted outbuilding belonging to the Priory Cottage in Northgate, Cottingham. The two or three horses needed to pull the machine were usually loaned by local benefactors.

Hull Royal Infirmary, Prospect Street, *c*.1915. Not all ambulances were painted white! This example seating six patients in bodywork adapted to a 20 h.p. Daimler chassis was painted the colour of deep blue. The driver of the waiting ambulance, accompanied by a nursing sister, look out across from the semi-circular driveway that ran in front of the Infirmary's main entrance.

Rolston Camp, near Hornsea, is the destination for a party of Hull Orderly Boys, pictured on the way to their annual summer camp, *c*.1921. Vehicles providing transport to the camp site include a Hull Corporation Highways Department Thornycroft loaded with camping equipment, followed by a pair of Hull Corporation Road Works Department's A.E.C. lorries carrying 80 or more Orderly Boys.

MISCELLANY

Manor Cars, Cowden. This eccentric-looking building, utilising open-top tramcar bodies as summer houses, was reputedly built by a retired Bradford wool merchant, c.1906. By the latter part of the 1920s, as a result of coast erosion, this unique house had disappeared.

The Northern Union rugby cup final for 1909, between Hull F.C. and Wakefield, was played at Headingley, Leeds. To commemorate the event, Wakefield Tramways decorated one of their open-topped tramcars with bunting and slogans which urged the home team to 'Gie Hull Wigin Lads.' The eventual result of the final was Hull F.C., Nil; Wakefield, 17.